LET GOD BE GOD

*Give Control to the Only
One Who Can Set You Free*

By Matthew D. Brough

LET GOD BE GOD

By Matthew D. Brough

CONTENTS

PART TWO: FAITH IS NOT A PROJECT

Reckoning Righteousness, Reckoning Grace
Romans 4

PART THREE: HAPPINESS, GENTLENESS, AND AN END TO ANXIETY

Learning From Philippians 4

Introduction

Trust No One. This was the tag-line of the television show The X-files, which premiered in 1993. It may as well have been the slogan of the last several generations. The trust in any authority, including politicians, our parents, and the majority of institutions, has eroded steadily since the 1960s.

Our lack of trust in anyone but ourselves does not stop at human authority, either. It extends beyond our earthly existence, and right to the throne of God almighty. Even in Christian churches, perhaps especially so, we have forgotten to trust God.

We've forgotten, and in some cases perhaps deliberately avoided trusting God, when, in fact, this trust is at the heart of Christianity. We are asked to believe, but we barely know what believing is anymore.

The X-files is an interesting illustration of our culture, because while it asked its characters to "trust no one" it also asked them to "believe." In this show, as in our culture, "belief" and "trust" were set up in competition to one another, but it is not supposed to be this way. "Belief" and "trust" are meant to go hand in hand. If someone trusts in God they obviously believe in God. If someone truly believes in God and acknowledges that God is good and is also really and truly God over everything (i.e. God is all-loving and all-powerful), then trusting God ought to follow.

The problem is it doesn't always follow. Most of us who claim to believe hold onto control of our lives far more tightly than Jesus ever wanted. Our desire for control over our own lives manifests itself in all kinds of ways. Even the most religious can end up using religion itself as a means of keeping control, rarely relinquishing it to God.

We may even try to control our relationship with God by turning it into something measurable and quantifiable. If we can just make sure we are reading the Bible enough, praying enough, going to church enough, then our faith will grow and we will be okay. All of those practices are very good things, but we can sometimes engage in them and never allow God the opportunity to work on us through them.

Instead, we keep ourselves safely in control even of our faith-life, careful to never let God in. We turn a relationship into a religion, and our practices become nothing more than systems, processes, and rules: the very things that Jesus, and then later the Apostle Paul, railed against as they spoke of God's amazing grace.

The breakdown of our trust in authority was not altogether a bad thing. What we have failed to recognize is that rather than replacing earthly authority with the only authority that can rightly claim our trust, we've quite wrongly placed ourselves at the center of things.

We have been taught to be self-sufficient, self-reliant, self-sustaining. This book seeks to disrupt that notion. My central assumption is that God is far more trustworthy than I am. I am better off trusting my life to God than I am trusting my life to me. I am far from self-sufficient, but God is all-sufficient.

This book is an attempt to help us see that we have generally put other things (quite often ourselves) in the place that only God can occupy. It is a small step to begin to stop "doing so much," and begin seeing what God is doing and has done.

As you are asked to let God be God, you are implicitly invited to think about how, in your own life, you are not allowing God to be God. Or another way of putting it, what's taking the place of God in your life?

PART ONE
Letting God Be In Charge

Of Kings, Apple Watches, and the Gods We Make For Ourselves
1 Samuel 8

1 / What Do You Want?

If you believe in God, you have probably at one time or another wanted something from God. If you're honest with yourself, you probably have a list of things right now. If you're not sure if you believe in God, you probably still have a list.

What do you want? Stop for a moment and really think about that question. Your list might include things like:

- Good health for yourself and your family
- A house
- A steady income
- Access to enough food and clean drinking water
- Indoor plumbing

Your list may also include:

- A vacation every year
- Netflix
- Season tickets to your local sports team

- A daily Starbucks visit

- A new car

We all want something.

Some people feel entitled. They dream of a certain kind of life, but can't quite figure out how to get it, often feeling like the world is conspiring against them, stopping them from attaining their dreams.

Other people take responsibility for their lives. They adopt a "pull yourself up by your bootstraps" attitude. They go to work to earn money to buy the life they think they want.

There are books for people who want to work hard for the life of their dreams. There are books for people who want to dream but not really lift a finger. This is neither of those books. This book is about stopping "the life you've always wanted" from becoming your god. This book is about ending the endless pursuit of whatever it is that you want most. It is about trusting God enough to let Him take charge of your life.

2 / If Only I Had...

Many of us have a general feeling of dissatisfaction with our lives. This may not on the surface appear as something all that terrible, and, at times it can be a motivator to action—to work on improving our lives. This feeling points to something true about ourselves as human beings. We long for something more, and often, something other than what we currently have.

We are excellent at placing the wrong things as objects of our longing. We falsely decide that our lives would become more complete if only we could possess something better than what we have. We decide it is easier to want the things of this earth than it is to put our trust in God for what we need, both materially and spiritually.

I love all things Apple. I always have. I did not jump on the bandwagon either. I was on board long before there were iPhones or even iPods. My family's first computer was an Apple

IIc, which came out in 1984. The only time I've ever owned a PC running Windows was when I was in college. I was broke, and I had to write papers, so I went and bought the cheapest computer I could find. I would regularly walk to the campus bookstore to drool over the shiny new bondi blue teardrop-shaped iMacs. I still follow Apple products and still watch the occasional product launch. Sadly, I sometimes covet my neighbor's Apple watch.

Being an Apple enthusiast means that I, like many others, have been persuaded that it is normal to love the product I have and also long for the next, better, version of that product yet to be released. Steve Jobs helped me uncover that little thrill when, in his product launches, he would say with a smile, "just one more thing." The crowd would cheer before he would even tell them what it was.

It's not just tech for me. It's also vacations. You know what I like to do on vacation? Dream about the next vacation. For you, it might be cars, or it might be your house, or renovation projects. Many of us have a sense that we will be happier "if only."

If only I had the latest tech.

If only I had a bigger house.

If only I had more money.

If only I can make it through to the next holiday.

If only I had more time to spend with my family.

Some "if onlys" can help you get motivated to work harder for the next promotion, or figure out how to organize your time better to get to your daughter's gymnastics meet. Often though, our dissatisfaction and its accompanying longing is unhealthy, though we rarely recognize it.

The ancient Hebrews were often dissatisfied, and sometimes rightly so. They endured slavery in Egypt, exile in Babylon, and foreign occupation. There were other times, however, when the people were dissatisfied and looked to the wrong places to fulfil that which they believed they were lacking. In other words, the ancient Hebrews played the "if only" game just like us.

One of these "if only" times shows up in the eighth chapter of the first book of Samuel. Samuel had been the people's leader. He had been acting as judge and arbiter when disputes arose. He was good at pointing to God as the one "in charge"— Samuel himself was a steward of the people of God, serving God and the people by preserving order. This is what a judge did in the time of the judges.

The people decided, however, that they didn't want to

simply have a judge. They wanted more than a steward. Samuel had been good at that job, but he was getting old and there was no obvious leader to take his place. The people asked for a king who would make them like other nations and who could go out and fight their battles for them.

Samuel objected to their request, telling the people what a king would really be like. "A king will enslave you," he said. "He will enlist you in a permanent army! He will tax you! He will take away all the best property and give it to his nobility."

When we examine this story, we are tempted to think it doesn't apply to us. We don't want a king. We want things like iPhones, vacations, nice houses, and healthy families. But please stick with the story.

It is important to understand that there is nothing inherently wrong with a monarchy, just as there is nothing inherently wrong with a house or an iPhone. What is wrong is when we put a human king, or a house, or a vacation, or even our family, in the place of that which will give us ultimate fulfillment or happiness. In short, we have a problem anytime we put something that is not God in the place of God.

3 / Following the Right Leader

As we follow this ancient story, we find that Samuel took the people's request as a rejection of his own leadership. They no longer wanted a judge—they wanted a king. We find, as well, that God saw the people's desire for a king as a rejection of His leadership. For God, it wasn't so bad that they didn't want Samuel as judge. It was far worse that they wanted a king other than the king they already had. You see, for the ancient Israelites, God was their king.

This summarizes one of our major human problems quite well. We don't want God to be king.

We must know something about how the ancient Israelites operated in the time of the judges. They had a God-given code of law, but people were essentially left to themselves in applying it. There was no centralized authority other than the priests. There was centralized religion, law, and heritage, but *enforcement* of the law was done by family, clan, and tribe.

The way the book of Judges tells it, when things got out of hand for the people, and they always did, God would allow a foreign enemy to take over the tribes of his own people. After a time, God would raise up a judge over all of Israel to save them, and to get people following the law again. This was usually accomplished through military conquest. The judge would bring the Israelites together to destroy an enemy who had moved in.

When the people asked for a king, they were asking for a permanent political nation that could be on the same playing field as, and stand up to, other nations.

The people wanted the security of a king to stop their foreign invasion problem. They wanted the institution of a nation so they could defend themselves against their enemies.

They wanted to treat a symptom, not find a cure. The symptom was foreign invasion, but the real problem was something deeper. Their desire for a king was just another symptom of the problem. The deeper problem was that they didn't want to trust God.

4 / A King or a Kingdom?

In some ways we all want kings. We don't think we do, but in reality, that is what we want. The people wanted a king who could fight their battles for them. They wanted something (or someone) to fix their life which was stuck in a pattern from which they seemed unable to escape.

We want that too. Give me something that will make my life better, or make me happier. We try to fix our lives with all kinds of things we would never call "kings." The irony is, those things often end up ruling us.

5 / Another Perspective

The books of Judges and Samuel tell the story in a particular way. We could tell it another way:

The people trusted God, but over time, they stopped relying on God. They stopped thinking they needed God. They started ignoring much of what God had asked them to do. They started behaving with contempt toward each other.

As time went on, peoples' lives were deteriorating. Even though they were one people, there were a lot of disputes, and people weren't treating each other fairly. People were divided along tribal lines, along family lines, and some families were even divided against themselves.

This made the Israelites easy pickings for foreign powers. One after another, throughout Israel's history, foreign enemies came in and took over. If only God's people had stuck with God, with the way of life God had given them, with loving and caring for one another, they would have remained strong.

Under foreign occupation, they had very few options left to them, so they cried out to God. Each time they did, God responded graciously by raising up a leader who could rally the people and set plans in motion to drive out the foreign occupying force. Surely once that happened, the people would remember God, remember their way of life, and go back to being the people God had intended them to be. But no, the cycle continued over and over again.

Finally, the people asked to have a king just like the other nations. That way they could defend themselves no matter what. They believed their real problem was the foreign enemies. They believed they needed a permanent, centralized leader with a permanent army to protect them, to keep their borders secure. Foreign enemies would no longer bother them.

In many ways, the request for a king meant putting a system in place that would allow for a better transition from leader to leader. Instead of the people waiting for God to raise someone up, they would have a built-in line of succession from the king to his son, and his son, and so on.

6 / A Different Kingdom

The people believed that the next thing would be awesome. They asked for a king so they could be like everyone else. They believed that having a king would fix everything. These reasons sound a lot like us. Why do I want a vacation, a house, or an Apple watch? Is it because other people have them? Is it because I think they will truly make my life better, or easier, or somehow make me happier?

As we follow the story in Samuel, we find that God gives in. God grants them a king. Why give in? Because in the end, the system of government doesn't matter. God didn't institute a system of government—God gave laws, but gave us complete freedom in how to organize ourselves. God's laws around things like foreign policy consist of interpersonal relationships. Most of the laws are either ritualistic/ceremonial, moral, or about how we treat each other. We find nothing about one system of government being superior to the other.

Another reason God gave them a king is that God always had a kingdom in mind. Kingdom is one of the best ways of describing what God is up to, because God is the one, true, supreme ruler.

We find that God's kingdom gets described in very different ways than human kingdoms. It is, however, a dominant metaphor for speaking about God's work. Jesus used kingdom language a lot! In Matthew, Mark, and Luke the word "kingdom" shows up in 116 different verses.

In John's gospel, however, it only shows up three times. John, generally doesn't use "kingdom" as a way of describing how we relate with God. John records Jesus saying things like "in my Father's house there are many rooms," or talking about himself as the shepherd of the sheep, or as being the vine and we being the branches. John leans toward connection imagery, rather than political imagery. This isn't to say that according to John, there isn't a kingdom. It's to say that we are using human language to describe a divine reality.

While John generally doesn't use the word, "kingdom" is in many cases a very helpful term. It tell us that we are subject to God. As we read through the New Testament, we find that Jesus, the great King, came and made himself subject to us, and asks us to be subject to one another. It is truly a different kind of kingdom.

7 / What's the Real problem?

The real problem is not really the King, or the system, it is the replacing of God with something else. It is misplacing our hope and our faith in a system, or a person, or a new technology, or the stock market, or whatever it is. That's the problem.

It's the replacing of God—and we've been doing it for a long time.

Not to muddy the waters too much, but we can see this in the now very old debate of science vs. God. There ought to be no debate about creation and evolution. Instead, the debate ought to be around where we place our hope and trust. If we honestly believe that the totality of the world's problems can be solved through better science and innovation, then we have replaced our savior with an idol of our own making.

That isn't to say that science or innovation are evil—far from it. What *is* evil, is our delusion that science and innovation can do what only God can do. It's not that a king over the kingdom of Israel was evil, it was the peoples' belief that if only they had a king like everyone else, then everything would be okay. In fact, everything can only be okay if God makes it okay. Our only hope is God, because only God is God. We can't let anything else become our ultimate hope. There is no other solution, there is no silver bullet.

8 / Ultimate Hope

Many have tried to do away with the idea of ultimate hope, or the idea of ultimate anything. But it's a very difficult thing to do away with. We can intellectually get rid of ultimate hope, but we still behave as though it's there.

Some place their ultimate hope in the economy. If the economy is on track, everything else will follow, they say. Having an ultimate hope also gives us something to ultimately blame. If something like health care is off track, the economist will be swift to point to an economic downturn. It won't matter too much who is elected to govern, except as a function of its effect on the economy. If the ultimate hope is a strong economy, then we will tend to have related personal goals, such as no debt, nice stuff, and disposable income, usually in the name of being able to provide a better life for our families.

Make no mistake, we have ultimate hopes, they are just so

often misplaced.

God is meant to be both ultimate hope and the ultimate goal. Sadly, the best we often do is make God into a piece of our equation for personal happiness. What a mess we are in.

9 / God's Gift Economy

How do we get out of the mess?

First, remember that God didn't say "no" to the people when they wanted a king. He found one for them, and their second king, David, became the model for what it meant to have a relationship with God. After David, God started using the language of kingdom to talk about the new reality that would one day come. Jesus used the language of the kingdom of God more than almost anything else. Some theologians have been using the idea of the economy of God to speak to us today, and I think some of that language is because we tend not to think in kingdoms anymore.

We need to realize that most of what we experience is not evil in and of itself. Rather, it is a gift. In a lot of ways, that is the key. God did *give* them a king, knowing that a whole bunch of the population was basically replacing God. God gave anyway.

God gives us wonderful things: science, technology, the ability to organize ourselves into democratic republics, health care systems, education systems, an economic system that allows us to employ millions in fairly meaningful work, so that families are fed, and social safety nets are created. None of them are perfect systems, but they are gifts. God gives amazing gifts.

10 / Our Mistreatment of God's Good Gifts

Over and over, we do two terrible things with the gifts that God gives:

1)   We denigrate and take for granted.

2)   We elevate them to the status of a god.

We rarely notice the second point because it is so embedded into our culture. Someone sings unbelievably well and we call them an idol. We learn so much about science that we, for at least the last 100 years or so, have been able to talk about the science vs. God debate, as though science and God are on the same playing field, and as though somehow human beings can be the referee in the debate.

What we forget to do, for the most part, is say thank you. Thank you, God, for the capacity to understand how electrons work. Thank you for giving us the ability to theorize about the origins of the universe. Thank you, God, for giving us a glimpse into the vast universe that you could hold in the palm of your hand. Thank you God for entertainment: for things like movies, for sport. Thank you for the ability you've given us to cure debilitating diseases. Thank you for educational systems. Thank you for hospitals, doctors, and nurses.

This list could go on and on, but generally, we take most of our lives for granted. That, or we complain about broken systems, moral decay in society, leniency in the criminal justice system, and the like.

These two human tendencies feed each other. We denigrate or take for granted. We don't say thank you, but complain. That leads to us looking for the ideal in the wrong place and raising it up as *the* solution. We believe that if only we could get to whatever ideal it is, then we'd fix its corresponding problem.

The solution becomes our hope and our goal, whether it is on a personal, national, or global scale. In effect, before we've even take a step, we already have an idol in mind. That is, we've replaced God with something else: some other thing, some other pursuit, or some other person.

11 / Fixing the Problem

We must first recognize that everything we have is a gift from God. Next, we say thank you.

Of course we should also try to make things better in our world, but we should only do that from a place of acknowledging that God has given everything.

This really addresses our denigration, our taking for granted, and our propensity for complaint. But what about our elevation of certain things to god status? How do we deal with placing our ultimate hope and faith in things other than God?

This is harder to do—it takes a real act of will.

Essentially, we are idolaters. We've replaced God with idols of our own making, whether government systems, or our jobs, or money, our technology, or even our families, or ourselves.

What we need to do is replace our idols. We've replaced God with other things, and now we need to replace those other things with God. (The idea of replacing our idols is best explained in Timothy Keller's excellent book *Counterfeit Gods*.)

Father, Son, and Spirit need to become both hope and goal in our lives. God needs to become our true King—the one over us, the one that occupies our thoughts, our hearts, and our lives.

Whenever something else is your hope, whenever something else is your solution, beware. Has it become an ultimate hope? Have you placed your trust in that thing? You can test this by asking yourself whether you often say these kinds of things...

- My problems will be done with once that promotion comes through.
- When I get in a relationship, I'll finally be happy.
- I'll be complete once I have children.
- I just need that vacation and I'll be okay.
- When I retire, I'll really start living.
- When I graduate, life is going to *really* start.

The Israelites asked for a king, because they believed it was going to be so much better. They were replacing God.

We must not allow anything to stand in the place of God in our lives. We must let God be in charge. We must let God be God.

Questions for Reflection or Discussion

1) What is on your "I want" list? What are some concrete ways you are placing items on this list ahead of God?

2) What "if only" do you regularly say to yourself? (e.g. If only I had more money) What could you say instead to remind yourself that all provision comes from God?

3) What do you think the following statement means? "We try to fix our lives with all kinds of things we would never call 'kings.' The irony is, those things often end up ruling us."

4) What are some ways that you are not allowing God to be sovereign in your life?

5) In what areas of life do you feel you are doing well in submitting to God as ruler?

6) What does it mean for God to be both ultimate hope and the ultimate goal? Contrast this with how we often treat God as only part of our equation for personal happiness.

7) What are some of the gifts God has given you in your life? What can you do to be more thankful on a regular basis?

8) How do you respond to the following statement?

"We've replaced God with other things, and now we need to replace those other things with God. Father, Son, and Spirit need to become both hope and goal in our lives. God needs to become our true King..."

How might you live this out in your own life?

PART TWO

Faith is Not a Project

Reckoning Righteousness, Reckoning Grace
Romans 4

12 / The Devastation of Earning Our Way

Sometimes it's really hard to get our heads around not having to earn our way. We have it ingrained in us.

- You reap what you sow.

- You can do anything you set your mind to.

- You can be anything you want to be.

- You need to be able to stand on your own two feet.

Our society is based on the idea that people should be working for a living to support themselves. These aren't bad ideas in and of themselves, but they are devastating when we apply them to relationships, especially our relationship with God.

13 / We Think God's Love is Contingent

Sadly, a lot of our human relationships are based on reciprocity and power. You scratch my back, I'll scratch yours. You build up loyalty and trust so that down the road you can call in favors. You have your favorite people, and you have people who really annoy you. You have friends and enemies. You have people who you'll forgive, and you have grudges that you're still holding. Respect must always be earned. When someone does what you want them to do, then you'll respond favorably to them.

This is how we are in so many of our human relationships, and so we think God is like that too. We think that God is waiting for us to be worthy. We think that God will respect us when we do what He wants us to do. We think that if God doesn't answer our prayers the way we want, then something is wrong either with us, or with God.

We think that God's love is contingent the way most of our love is contingent—even though we know it's not supposed to be that way.

14 / You Gotta Have Faith

We have to out-think our normal way of thinking. We need to embrace that our right-ness with God, our righteousness, is not based on our worthiness or how good we are. It is not based on our actions.

> *Therefore, since we are justified by faith, we have peace with God through our Lord Jesus Christ. —Romans 5:1*

We are taught using the above scripture (and also primarily Ephesians 2:8) that it is faith, not works, that justify, save, or make us righteous. Faith, not works, will secure your place with God. Faith, not works, will make you right with God.

There is nothing you can do to *earn* righteousness with God. As much as we try to do something, to earn, to reciprocate for what God has done, none of that is necessary, nor will it work. Only faith can bring you a right relationship with God.

15 / Be Like Abraham

The Apostle Paul spends an inordinate amount of time building to Romans 5:1. Almost all of the fourth chapter of Romans appears to be Paul asking us to be like Abraham in our faith.

We are told that "Abraham believed God, and it was reckoned to him as righteousness." (Romans 4:3)   In other words, God saw not the works Abraham was doing, not his obedience to the law, but his faith, his heart. And when God saw Abraham's heart, he counted that as him being righteous. Abraham's faith became the basis of him being right with God, rather than anything Abraham did.

You can argue that Abraham's faith was displayed through his actions, but Paul, in Romans 4 looks at Genesis 15, and seems to say that all of Abraham's good works flowed from his faith. All of Abraham's good deeds, all of his following the law, all of his obedience was only an outcropping of his faith, by which he was already justified.

So, be like Abraham, we are told. Believe like him, and you too will be made righteous.

16 / The Task of Faith

There is something wonderfully good about the idea of our righteousness being based on faith. It frees us from the power of sin. Even though we mess up, even though we've done things we are ashamed of, even though we keep trying and failing, with faith, God still justifies us. God continues loving us, and sets us right with him.

If it depended on our actions, we'd all be in trouble. If it depended on how much good we did in our lives or if we had to measure up to a certain standard, that would be terrifying.

This is good news theology. It takes all the emphasis from our very flawed actions, and places all the emphasis on faith. It reminds us that God does not count our sins against us. Instead, God looks into our hearts.

It also means that we cannot judge anyone on the basis of what we see them do. Only God is in the position to make a judgement. Only God can see a person's heart and know their faith.

This is all wonderfully good from a human point of view, because it frees us from our sinful actions and it does something else for us as well. Something that we all want, something we crave.

It gives us a nice project to work on. Faith is our project. There's still a nice big task. You've got to have faith, build faith, get faith. Be like Abraham.

17 / But What If My Faith is Deficient?

What if I don't have faith? Or what if my faith isn't like Abraham's? I mean, are we really talking about having the same *level* of faith as Abraham?

The story Paul references in Romans 4 is about Abraham in his golden years. God promised him that he would be the Father of many nations, that his wife Sarah, at age 90, would have a son. Abraham believed God. What if I don't have that kind of faith? What if my faith wavers? Then what?

The problem is that we've often made faith itself into a work, an action, or a possession. Faith easily becomes something to be quantified. It is something to be proud of when it appears strong. It is something to be ashamed of when it feels weak.

We say things like:

- "my faith gives me energy to get through my week." Or...

- "I'm so glad I have my faith to get me through tough times." Or...

- "I don't know what I'd do without my faith."

What if you go through a difficult time and you feel like your faith is letting you down? Or what if you get to the end of your week and you are just spent, or you're spiralling into a depression?

Is your faith deficient then? And does a deficient faith, along with other problems you might be experiencing, set you on the outside of righteousness?

18 / Frame of Reference for Faith

The problem with measuring faith is that there is no frame of reference. If I tell you to have faith like Abraham did, I could be talking about all kinds of things. Does that mean, have a faith that enables you to do the kind of things that Abraham did? Does that mean believe the words that you think you hear God telling you, just like Abraham believed what God said? Does it mean something else entirely?

19 / Stop. Who Are We Talking About?

Let's stop here.

Have you noticed that most of this discussion hasn't really been about God? It has actually been about us.

We like to talk about ourselves. We like to think about ourselves. We like things that are about us or that help solve *our* problems.

It turns out that most of our ideas about faith, center much more around ourselves than they do around God.

We wonder about the level of our faith in the same way we wonder whether we are worthy of God's love. We easily make it all about *our* faith, and how God looks at *our* hearts and then sets *us* right depending on what He finds there.

We so easily give ourselves a project, or make ourselves into the project.

20 / Faith Is About Its Subject

The subject of faith is God, and that is what is most important. It's not really your faith that gets you through difficult times—it's God.

In John 20:26-29 we read about the disciple Thomas who refuses to believe that Jesus is risen from the dead, even though all of the other disciples told him they had seen Jesus. Thomas tells the other disciples, "Unless I see the mark of the nails in his hands, and put my finger in the mark of the nails and my hand in his side, I will not believe." (John 20:25)

A week goes by before Jesus comes to his disciples again, and this time Thomas is with them. We gloss over the fact that a week goes by, but just try to imagine that week for Thomas! He has made a declaration that he will not believe, yet he stays with his friends. What did the other disciples think about Thomas? Surely, all week they would have all been talking about the risen

Jesus.

I imagine Thomas being conflicted about his declaration of "I won't believe." I imagine him wishing he could believe, but just not being able to. I also imagine the other disciples harboring judgment against Thomas. Would they have thought him deficient in some way because he did not have faith?

There is no such judgement when Jesus confronts Thomas. Really, we can barley call it a confrontation. Jesus stands in front of Thomas and says "Put your finger here and see my hands. Reach out your hand and put it in my side. Do not doubt but believe." (John 20:27) Jesus gives Thomas exactly what he needs in order to have his faith rebuilt.

In the end, the Thomas story isn't really about Thomas' doubts or faith, it is about Jesus and what he does for Thomas. Thomas goes from a deficient faith to full faith, but it really has nothing to do with his own will. Thomas doesn't do anything to get his faith back. It is the Lord Jesus who restores Thomas' faith. The point here is that it isn't faith itself that is the most important thing. It is Jesus, God, the One who is the subject of faith, that is.

Certainly, subjectively or psychologically, your faith helps you. But isn't it God Himself, not your faith in God, who rescues you, provides for you, and sets you free? It's not your faith that gives you energy to get through your week, as though your act of believing is somehow triggering a kind of spiritual nutrient. If anything is getting you through your week, it is the almighty and all-loving God.

In other words, it's not about you.

21 / All About God

If we set ourselves a project of having faith and we use Abraham's faith as our yardstick, we are going to be trouble. We might as well go back to trying to win God's approval by keeping all the commandments, or living a life full of good deeds. Abraham's faith was off the charts, if there is a chart.

But here is what we need to realize. Abraham's faith wasn't about Abraham. Abraham's faith was about God.

In Romans 4:17, Paul lays out the importance of the subject of faith.

"He (Abraham) is our father in the sight of God, in whom he believed—the God who gives life to the dead and calls into being things that were not." (NIV)

Is this about how great Abraham's faith is, or is this about the God who gives life to the dead and creates things out of nothing? Even if it were the faith in our hearts that makes us righteous in God's sight (and I'm not convinced of this!), who cares about that, when compared to the overwhelming reality that God makes the dead live and creates entire worlds simply by speaking.

How did our hearts and minds develop in the first place? Who made us predisposed to faith? Who created us? Who knew us before we were even born? Who knows us intimately? Who could tell you the number of grains of sand on every single beach? Who can comprehend the depth of the universe? Who could, if He wanted to, hold that universe in His hand and describe to you what is beyond it?

What are we thinking when we make it about *our* faith giving us enough energy to get through our week?

Our faith isn't supposed to be about us at all.

22 / Will, Power, and High Stakes Trusting

Abraham believed what God told him because he was fully persuaded that God had the power to do what He had promised. Implicit here is that Abraham believed that God also *wanted* to do what He had promised. Abraham believed that God had the will and the power to follow through.

When someone promises you something, and you believe that they have the will and the power to follow through on their promise, you are trusting them. And the stakes go up with the nature of the promise.

Imagine that a friend promises that they will meet you tomorrow for lunch at your favorite restaurant. They are probably going to be there. They are your friend, you trust them. The stakes are pretty low. It's just lunch.

Imagine a different someone making a different kind of promise. This someone promises to remain faithful to you: to love, honor and cherish you, in richer and poorer, in health and sickness, in plenty and in poverty. There are not a lot of people you would choose to trust if they said those words to you. We tend to only trust one person with that kind of promise. The stakes are high. It is marriage, after all.

In the story we are following, someone promises Abraham that his descendants will be as many as the stars, that kings will be among them, and that nations will come from his offspring. This promise comes to him when he is close to 100 years old and he has no children. The stakes are massive. Only God has the ability to pull this off. God is the only one to trust with this. The question for Abraham is, does he *trust* God?

Someone promises you eternal life. Someone promises you that, because of his son dying on a cross and rising again, none of your misdeeds count against you, and you will participate in his everlasting reign when he rules over all creation as Lord and King. Someone promises you that there is a time coming when all things will be set right: when there will be an end to suffering, violence, and oppression, and where every tear will be wiped away.

There is only one someone who can pull this off.

The question is, do you trust that someone?

23 / So, Are We Saved By Faith?

The core of it all is not simply believing so that you can "get righteousness." It's trusting God, believing that God can and will follow through on it all.

When I believe just to get the benefits, that isn't actually trusting in God. That is trusting in my own ability to have faith. When I believe just to get the benefits, I am believing that my faith is saving me.

But what is wrong with that? you might ask.

You will hear that we are "saved by faith," but this isn't quite right and, even though you will find that shorthand in the Bible, it's not the complete picture. We are saved by grace *through* faith.

In other words, our salvation does not derive from our own internal power of believing in God. Our salvation is based solely on what God has graciously done for us in Christ. Our faith is about trusting that God has both the power and the will to follow through on what God has begun in us through Christ.

24 / Pointing to Outlandish Grace

When Paul wrote Romans, he was not trying to make faith into another kind of work or another kind of law. He was not trying to say that God is "up there" waiting to see if you *really* believe before he credits your righteousness account or before he saves you.

Paul was writing to people who already believed. He was trying to tell them something revolutionary in religion and in life. It is still revolutionary, so much so that even those in the Church don't quite live it out. We're good at setting projects, goals, tracking numbers, and the like. We aren't so good at heeding what Paul was saying.

Contrary to what anyone else might have told the Roman Christians, or us, Paul asserts that, as people who believe, we are people who should know that there is nothing required of us —that God has already taken care of it.

Paul wasn't trying to say that faith is the only requirement. They already *did* believe. He was telling them that they too shared in the promises to Abraham, that they were just as much Abraham's children as anyone else. They too were counted as righteous even when their actions were not always right. We too receive this kind of reckoning—not because we believe perfectly, or in a particularly way—not really *because* of our faith at all.

> The words "it was credited to him" were written not for him alone, but also for us, to whom God will credit righteousness—for us who believe in him who raised Jesus our Lord from the dead. He was delivered over to death for our sins and was raised to life for our justification. Romans 4:23-25

The emphasis is not on how we *have to* believe in order to "get righteousness" from God. The emphasis is on what God will do for us who believe already, and what God has already done in justifying us through the death and resurrection of Jesus.

Our faith doesn't point to our abilities to gain our own salvation. No, our faith always points to the outlandish grace of God, whose promises and gifts go far beyond anything we could accomplish by works or by faith.

25 / Receiving

In my tradition we baptize infants. You may belong to a church that doesn't do that, but may have baby dedications. In either case, this moment is an amazing display of God's grace. When a child is presented to God for baptism or dedication, we can't point to the power of her action or her faith as a basis for her relationship with God. She is totally dependent on God for that.

The baby is claimed as God's child. The church proclaims that she is part of God's covenant of grace, that she is as much one of Abraham's descendants as anyone else, that she is a recipient of God's promises alongside all the saints that have gone before.

None of this is the baby's own doing, nor is it the Church's, or even the parents. The child's inheritance in God's kingdom, her justification through the death and resurrection of Christ, her righteousness, is given completely through the grace of God, which we pray she will one day receive and claim for herself in faith, by the power of the Holy Spirit.

As a baby is presented for baptism or dedication, he very well might receive God's grace more perfectly than at any time in life. The grace of God is given and the child simply receives, though he won't remember it.

If only we could all receive so easily.

We almost always jump to *what do I have to do?* Or we ask, am *I good enough?* Or, *is my faith strong enough?*

But this is all a gift. It is all God's grace.

Jesus went to the cross and rose again for you. That is a done deal—an unimaginable gift.

Your faith is not about earning or measuring. It is not about reciprocity. God isn't paying you back for believing and you can never pay God back for what he's done for you.

All you can do is place your trust in the Lord your God, who does, in fact, have the power and the will to make you righteous in Christ.

Questions for Reflection or Discussion

1) Why is "earning your way" such a problem when it comes to relationships, and especially a relationship with God?

2) In what ways to you behave as though God's love is conditional?

3) When have you tried to earn God's love or favor through your actions?

4) Have you ever turned faith itself into a project? Have you "used" faith to earn God's love?

5) Do you talk about relying on your faith more than you talk about relying on God? If so, why do you think you phrase it this way?

6) In what ways have you kept yourself at the center of your ideas about faith and kept God from being the true focus of your faith?

7) Think about the promises of God: eternal life, unconditional love, forgiveness, the coming kingdom of peace where all suffering and even death will be no more. What are the stakes in trusting the One who has promised all of this? What is it about God that makes you willing to trust Him?

8) How do you respond to the following statement?
"When I believe just to get the benefits, that isn't actually trusting in God. That is trusting in my own ability to have faith. When I believe just to get the benefits, I am believing that my faith is saving me."
What is wrong with believing just to get the benefits?

9) Is there a difference between being "saved by faith" and being "saved by grace through faith?"

10) Reflect on the following: "We almost always jump to what do I have to do? Or we ask, am I good enough? Or, is my faith strong enough? But this is all a gift. It is all God's grace." Do you believe this? Do you trust God?

PART THREE

Happiness, Gentleness, and an End to Anxiety

Learning From Philippians 4

26 / Always Be Happy?

Rejoice in the Lord always; again I will say, Rejoice! —Philippians 4:4

Does anyone rejoice always? I know I don't. Is it even possible? We think this verse reads "Rejoice always," as though we are being given a command to produce our own joy.

The verse does not command us to "rejoice always." It says, "Rejoice *in the Lord* always." This verse is talking about Jesus.

Part of our problem is that we tend to want to rejoice in all kinds of other things with no reference to Jesus or God or the Holy Spirit.

We also tend to disconnect this verse from what follows in Philippians 4, yet this particular passage provides us with some keys to joy, gentleness, overcoming worry, and gaining inner peace. Sound good? Then let's heed the words of Philippians 4.

27 / What Are You Known For?

Let your gentleness be known to everyone. The Lord is near. —
Philippians 4:5

I really wish this verse said "let your sarcasm be known to everyone." I would be doing well. But gentleness? Really?

Some people may think that the verse ought to read "let your sadness be known to everyone," or "let your anger be known to everyone," or "let your frustration be known to everyone." I'm convinced that, given their social media presence, some people think this verse ought to read "let what you ate for lunch be known to everyone."

This verse seems to asks the question, "What are you known for?" Are you known for gentleness? With this question comes a not so subtle command. We are more likely to hear this verse as an order from on high: Be gentle!

It is okay to strive to be obedient to God—to be gentle because the Lord told us to. It is also okay and perhaps helpful to ask ourselves whether we are known for gentleness. However, when we approach this verse in this way, we once again miss the whole point.

Much like verse 4, where we forget about the "in the Lord" part of the command to "rejoice," here we also tend to overlook the second part of the verse. We focus on "let your gentleness be know to everyone" but, to our great detriment, ignore "the Lord is near."

28 / Strong Gentleness

Why is gentleness linked with the Lord being near?

It's not that Jesus will judge you for not being gentle. This isn't about watching out for your behavior. This is about how the nearness of Jesus provides the possibility for your gentleness to be known. If you are spending time with Jesus, you will get angry at injustice from time to time, but you shouldn't get more cranky.

The outward expression of Jesus' nearness to you will be a kind and gentle spirit.

This doesn't mean being a push-over. It does mean loving people. It does mean not trampling over people. It does mean caring about others. It does mean taking the time to listen and understand someone. It does mean suspending judgment about someone. It does mean asking God to take away your prejudices, to take away your hatred, to put an end to grudges and bitterness.

This verse is meant to be encouraging, not a hardship.

The source of your gentleness is not you—it's Jesus, so take heart. You *can* be gentle, you *can* be loving, you *can* display compassion and forgiveness, because the Lord is near. It does not depend on your power, your will, or your abilities. It depends on the Lord Jesus.

This verse is not simply a command to be gentle. It is certainly not a command to be weak. It is an encouragement that you can be powerfully gentle with others. You can have a strong kindness, because the Lord is near. Be encouraged in this. The Lord is near.

Do you believe he is near to you? He is. Jesus is right there, by the working of the Holy Spirit. The Lord is near, wanting to work in you, with all power and authority, for you to be kind, loving, and compassionate. Gentle.

29 / Don't Worry, Pray Instead

Do not worry about anything, but in everything by prayer and supplication with thanksgiving let your requests be made known to God. — Philippians 4:6

Have you ever heard someone say "Don't worry?" How about "Just pray about it?" I used to get really mad at people who said things like that. It always sounded so trite to me. I wonder sometimes, though, if some of "those people" have a deeper faith than I ever will. Some of them seriously pray from the depths of their souls through the deepest of pain. Many of them have a quiet faith that, when translated into words, comes out simply as "just pray about it."

We can, however, take a verse like the one above and, just like the two before it, make it into something that we are *supposed to do*. Here is what we can often think these verses

BCPL checkout

Call number: 248.4
Bro
Author: Brough,
Matthew D.,
Title: Let God be God :
give control to the
only one who
Due Date: 21 June
2017 23:59

Total checkouts for
session:1
Total checkouts:1

say on a surface level.

Verse 4—We're supposed to always rejoice.

Verse 5—We're supposed to be gentle all the time.

Verse 6—We're not supposed to worry. We should just pray.

30 / So, What Should I Do?

We are a bit obsessed with what we should do. The question of what we should do shows up throughout Scripture.

In Luke chapter 3, John the Baptist was preaching a major fire and brimstone sermon. He starts by calling his audience, or his congregation, a brood of vipers. He starts his sermon with "you're a bunch of snakes!" He tells them that they should be bearing fruit worthy of repentance.

We sometime get hung up on a word like repentance. At its heart, it means turn around, change of mind, change of heart, or change of attitude. We often mistakenly think repentance only means putting our actions right, but repentance is actually about interior change. Repentance is an interior action.

People were going to John and being baptized in the river, dipped in the waters for repentance. The washing in the water was an outward sign of an interior action. They were declaring in an outward way that their hearts and minds were turned back to God.

But John calls them all snakes. Why? Because a lot of them are just trying to cover themselves. If they do all the right religion, they think they will be okay. If they participate in the signs and symbols of the heart they think they will be fine. John says no. He says, "bear fruit worthy of repentance." In other words, we can know if the interior change of repentance has really happened by looking at your actions. You've got to match your actions to the interior change that you are claiming, to the repentance you are pointing to with your baptism.

A lot of the people listening to John were moved by his words. I think many actually did want their actions to match the interior change they had claimed. A lot of us are like that. We *want* to do better. We have conviction in our hearts, yet our actions don't always measure up to what we say we believe, or what we want to believe.

When John told them that they needed to bear fruit, that their actions needed to match the inner change of repentance, the crowd asked their question: "What then should we do?" (Luke 3:10) What are those actions? What does it look like to bear fruit? That's what we want to know. What are the 10 steps? What do I have to do?

John answers in a pretty basic way. "Whoever has two coats must share with anyone who has none; and whoever has food must do likewise." (Luke 3:11) Some specific people come forward. Tax-collectors come to John and ask, "what should we do?" He doesn't say, "quit your job and devote your life to God." He says, "don't cheat people." Roman soldiers ask what they should do. John tells them to be satisfied with their wages and not to extort money. This is pretty basic stuff.

People wondered if maybe John was the Messiah, but John would have none of that. He told them that Jesus was coming. While John dipped them in water as a symbol of their inner change, the powerful Messiah, Jesus, was coming to dip them in the Holy Spirit and fire.

In the end, John's message wasn't about what you should do at all. His message was "Get ready! Jesus is about to do something to you and in you that me and my water and my message could never do. The real one with the real power is still coming. Get ready for him."

John's message wasn't about giving people practical advice on bearing fruit. John was preparing them for something that God was about to do in them. The primary message was about

God. And somehow we miss it. We make it all about "me."

We still ask "what should I do?" when the answer is "God is doing something."

31 / It's Actually About What God is Doing

We do this with much of the Bible. We read it for guidance on what *I* should do. We therefore miss that passages like Philippians 4 are actually much more about what God is going to do.

When we read Philippians 4 we might think two things:

1) This is dumb. It's not real life. No one can always rejoice. No one can be known by everyone for their gentleness. It's impossible not to worry at least some of the time.

Or:

2) If only I could do this, my life would be better. I just have to try harder to rejoice, and be gentle, and I've got to just pray about things more and then I won't worry so much. I wish I didn't have such trouble with that. I don't know how these *really* good Christians do it. If only I was a better Christian, a better person.

These approaches both miss that this passage isn't about whether we can do these things or not. This passage is about God.

Verse 4: "Rejoice *in the Lord* always." It won't happen without God.

Verse 5: "Let your gentleness be known to everyone. *The Lord is near.*" You can be consistently gentle with people because God is close by, enabling you to do that.

Verse 6: "Do not worry," but do what? Take everything to God in prayer.

32 / Prayer and the Challenge of Worry

Verses six and seven seem to me to be the real kicker. This is the one I think we have the most trouble with. I know I do. Don't worry about anything. Don't worry about anything? How is that even possible?

Listen to how universal these verses are.

"...but in *everything* by prayer and supplication with thanksgiving let your requests be made known to God." (Philippians 4:6)

I worry a lot. I worry about all kinds of things. I also pray about those things, usually a lot. It took me a long time, however, before I realized that I wasn't really praying in the way this verse is talking about prayer.

So many of my prayers were about asking God for "help." Some of my prayers were bargains that I was trying to make with God and I was never particularly bold in praying for what I really longed for.

I would pray prayers asking God to "help someone get better" rather than praying for complete healing through the power of the Holy Spirit. I would pray prayers like "God, if you just help me get through this busy season, then I'll do better in serving you," rather than praying boldly for God to eliminate stress.

But the problems of timidity and bargaining paled by comparison to the fact that my prayer life generally centered around the list of things I wanted rather than around God as someone with whom I had a relationship. We must remember that prayer is the primary way we work on our relationship with God. When we think of a human example, it puts our prayer life into perspective.

Imagine if all your conversations with the person you love most in the world focussed solely on what you wanted that person to do for you. The relationship would be over very quickly. Should we still ask? Of course—but the asking cannot be the basis of the relationship. If you are going to ask someone to do something and it cuts right to the core of who you are, right to the deepest desires of your heart, then you better trust that person. Trust is the bedrock of bold prayer.

Think also about people facing major crises. Think of people who have lost their homes and their family members because of a Hurricane or other natural disaster, or people who have been the victims of abuse or other kinds of violence. Most of those people are crying out to God. I don't think many of them are praying, "God, I just need a bit of help to figure this out." Wouldn't most of them be praying, "God do something?" Many of them are entrusting their families to God, putting their trust in God, because they are living with a sense of desperation.

It would be naive to say that the simple act of praying the right kind of prayer, a prayer that *displays* trust, will get rid of your worry or your fear. It won't for people in these desperate situations. So, what will?

It's not a question of what, it's a question of who.

33 / Trust God Because He's God

This isn't about praying the right prayer. It's about actually placing your trust in God to sort things out.

This doesn't mean you won't do any work yourself. It doesn't mean you stop studying for exams, or that you quit a job that you don't like. It means that you entrust whatever it is that is causing worry and fear to God, and you don't do that act of entrusting just so that you can feel less worried or fearful.

You do that act of entrusting because that is treating God as God. That is believing that God and only God has the power to see the entire picture and do what is right and what is needed. Entrusting God is believing that only God can sort out the mess of evil and suffering.

We entrust whatever it is to God, because God is Lord, God is the ruler of creation, only God is God.

34 / Peace Beyond Understanding

As we start to wrap our minds around truly trusting God in prayer, we get Philippians 4:7 and it blows us away. When, instead of worrying, you really believe that God can handle it, when you trust God, when you do surrender and allow God to be God in your life, verse 7 happens.

And the peace of God, which surpasses all understanding, will guard your hearts and minds in Christ Jesus. —Philippians 4:7

This is so cool.

How does the worry get taken away, fully and completely? How does the fear disappear? We don't know. There isn't a simple correlation here. It isn't the praying of the right prayer.

The peace that we receive from God surpasses all understanding. We have no idea how it arrives. It is mysterious.

Are you worried about something? Go and pray. Give

everything over to God. Let it all go. Trust God enough to give God everything. That takes a lot of trust. Whatever it is in your life right now, give it to God and actually trust God with it. Don't let it be yours anymore. Pray that prayer.

Do that, but don't expect that you will receive peace because you've prayed that way. Peace will come kind of out of left field. It's a peace that no one understands. It's a peace that comes only from God, and it protects your changed heart. This is the true inner change that John the Baptist was talking about. It comes more from the Holy Spirit than it does from us.

Our step is simply trusting God. It is being willing to take your greatest worry, greatest fear, and believe that God actually can and will do what is necessary to be done with you.

35 / Trust

None of this is about what you should do. Don't create a "be better at trusting in God" project for yourself. Instead, know that God will do something in you and with you. Know that God is up to something in this world, and will in the end overcome all pain and suffering and evil.

If you do need something to do, give your greatest worry and fear over to God. And then wait. Wait for what's next from your Creator, Redeemer and Sustainer. Wait for the Protector and Provider, the One who loves you more than you can know, the One who laid down his life for you. Wait for the crucified and risen One, the One who has the power to do far more than you could ever ask or imagine.

Jesus has already imagined what he wants to do in your life. Trust.

Questions for Reflection or Discussion

1) How is rejoicing in the Lord different than just rejoicing? What other things do you rejoice in? How might you rejoice in the Lord more?

2) What are you known for? How might you let God work in you so that you are known more for gentleness?

3) How do you understand "strong gentleness?"

4) What are some of your causes for worry or anxiety?

5) Do you think our propensity for action (always wanting to do something) adds to our worry? How might you trust that God is taking action instead of asking "what should I do?"

6) What do you think "trust is the bedrock of bold prayer" means? How is your prayer life contributing to the development of your trust in God?

7) What do you find challenging about the idea of actually trusting God to sort things out? What do you find comforting about this idea?

8) Have you ever experienced a peace that passes understanding? If so, write down or think about what it was like. If not, try to imagine letting go of your anxiety and giving it over to God. Try praying the prayer where you actually trust God with your life.

9) What are the greatest obstacles you have to trusting in God (allowing God to be God in your life)? What steps do you think you need to take to allow God to truly be God in your daily life?

Find Out More…

Thank you for reading *Let God Be God*. There are more Let God Books for you to read, and you can find more books, articles, and other great things at my website, mattbrough.com. There, you can sign up to receive free exclusive content and you can find links to my facebook page, where I post devotional videos and other fun (and hopefully helpful) stuff!

I'm also the author of a series of fantasy books for young readers, though many adults enjoy them as well. You can find out all about that series on the website.

I'm always happy to hear from readers, so feel free to reach out. Just visit mattbrough.com to be in touch!

Peace,

Matthew Brough

Other *Let God* Books

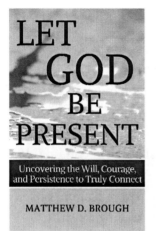

Let God Be Present
Uncovering the Will, Courage, and Persistence to Truly Connect

What does it really mean to connect with God? We search for meaning, connection, or guidance, but rarely let go of our pre-conceived notions of what we want to hear. This book asks you to trust God to be present and speak on His terms, rather than insisting that God fit in with your own idea of what He should be doing in your life.

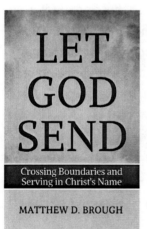

Let God Send
Crossing Boundaries and Serving in Christ's Name

God sends each follower of Jesus to serve others. The way we serve might be in small and simple ways, but God also tends to stretch us, moving us beyond the easy and across boundaries that we wouldn't always wish to cross. Not a how-to guide, this book is a thought provoker for anyone serious about following Christ, who wonders how to keep serving over a lifetime of faith.

All of the proceeds from this book are being donated to two ministries that work primarily with Canada's First Nations people.

Winnipeg Inner City Missions

Winnipeg Inner City Missions is committed to providing a healthy community for children, youth and families living in Winnipeg's Inner City.

The North End of Winnipeg is a challenging environment for families trying to raise their children to stay out of gangs and away from drugs, alcohol and negative influences. This is why this organization focuses on healing and reconciliation, poverty reduction, access to equal opportunities, striving towards excellent education standards and encouraging our children and youth towards higher learning and safe living.

Kenora Fellowship Centre

The Kenora Fellowship Centre offers shelter and comfort to the vulnerable, the disadvantaged and the displaced. It is the only operation giving refuge from the streets to the marginalized citizens within the community and is strategically located in downtown Kenora. All are extended a warm welcome, a cup of coffee or tea, a snack, and often a warm meal.

Both of these ministries are supported by and are missions of The Presbyterian Church in Canada.

CPSIA information can be obtained
at www.ICGtesting.com
Printed in the USA
LVOW10s1545230317
528244LV00010B/1234/P